For Wisler
—P.M.

For Gulala and Omer
—M.B.

To Kelsey and Dan
—Y.I.

Balzer + Bray is an imprint of HarperCollins Publishers.

The Bicycle: How an Act of Kindness Changed a Young Refugee's Life
Text copyright © 2024 by Patricia McCormick and Mevan Babakar
Illustrations copyright © 2024 by Yas Imamura
All rights reserved. Manufactured in Italy.
No part of this book may be used or reproduced in any manner whatsoever without
written permission except in the case of brief quotations embodied in critical articles
and reviews. For information address HarperCollins Children's Books, a division of
HarperCollins Publishers, 195 Broadway, New York, NY 10007.
www.harpercollinschildrens.com

Library of Congress Control Number: 2023942530
ISBN 978-0-06-305699-2

The artist used gouache, watercolor, and crayons to create the illustrations for this book.
Typography by Dana Fritts
24 25 26 27 28 RTLO 10 9 8 7 6 5 4 3 2 1
First Edition

THE BICYCLE

HOW AN ACT OF KINDNESS CHANGED
A YOUNG REFUGEE'S LIFE

WRITTEN BY
Patricia McCormick & Mevan Babakar

ILLUSTRATED BY
Yas Imamura

BALZER + BRAY
An Imprint of HarperCollins Publishers

When Mevan was a little girl, she lived in a land where figs fell from the trees and the air smelled like honeysuckle.

In the morning, she'd wake to the sound of the rooster crowing. And in the evening, she'd fall asleep to the sound of the frogs peeping.

Each day, she'd recite a little bit of poetry. To her mother, who clapped her hands. To her father, who kissed her forehead.

To her aunts and uncles, who pinched her cheeks. To her grandmother, who hugged her tight. To her grandfather, who hugged her tighter.

And to the grocer, who gave her a sweet.

Kurdistan, a lush and hilly corner in the north of Iraq,
was her home. Her family had always lived here.

Not just her parents. Her parents' parents. Her parents' parents' parents. Her parents' parents' parents' parents. And while Mevan may have been the littlest girl in her family, the love all around her made her feel ten feet tall.

But the ruler of Iraq had always made the people in Kurdistan feel like they didn't belong. Soon, Kurds were being punished for speaking their own language. Or using their Kurdish names. Or celebrating their holidays.

Then he sent soldiers to force them out of their homes.
And helicopters to push them into the mountains.

Mevan's parents were heartbroken. But they packed their bags and left.

They left behind Mevan's beloved aunts and uncles, the grandparents and the grocer. As she waved goodbye to all the people she loved, Mevan made herself very small.

Her family took a van to Turkey, a country on the other side of the mountains. As people squeezed into the van, Mevan made herself even smaller.

But the people wouldn't let them stay there. So, her family took a plane to Azerbaijan, a country even farther away. As people boarded the plane, Mevan made herself teeny tiny.

But the people wouldn't let them stay there either. So, her family took a train through forests and fields, across rivers and mountains and plains. For three days, Mevan hid in a train car, making herself almost invisible.

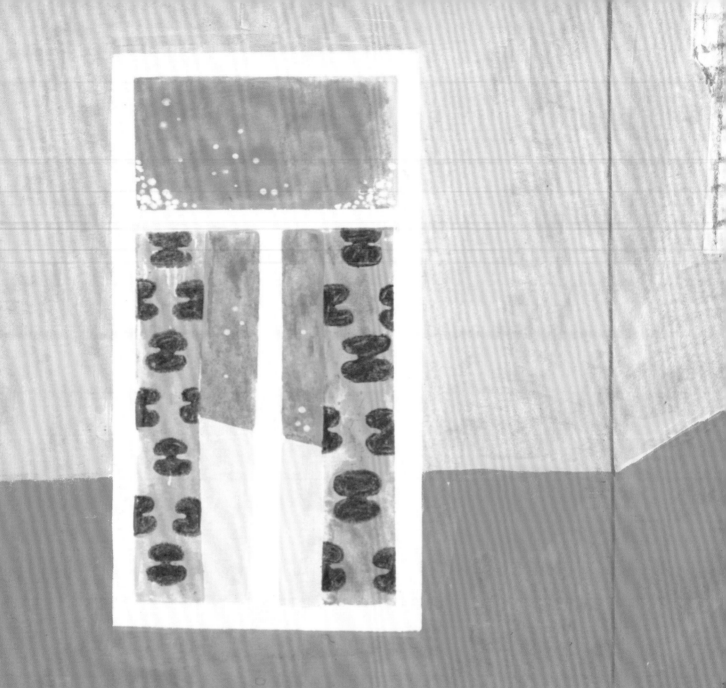

Russia was a cold, snowy place, but at least they could stay for a while if they hid.

There were no aunts and uncles, no grandmother, no grandfather. And no grocer to give her a sweet. There was hardly enough money for food. And no money at all for toys.

Mevan watched the children in Russia play outside on their sleds. She watched them play with their dolls. But they didn't invite her to join them. Because she was different here too.

They would point and stare and make fun of her because of the color of her skin or because her hair was different. Now Mevan wished she *was* invisible.

After two long years, her family had finally saved enough money to leave Russia. They flew to the Netherlands, a green and bright country, where the people told her family they could stay until they found a real home.

They gave them an apartment in a tall building with other families who'd been forced to leave their homes. They even gave Mevan ice cream after dinner.

But Mevan hid in her apartment and just watched the people from her window. They all buzzed around town on something she'd never seen before: a bicycle. The grown-ups rode them to go to work. The mail carriers rode them to deliver the mail. And the children rode them everywhere. Mevan wished she could go outside and join them, but she'd gotten so good at making herself small she thought no one would notice her.

But while she was looking out the window,
someone was looking out for her.

It was Egbert, the man who fixed things in the building where she lived. His job was to take care of the building, but he was a kind man who also took care of the people inside it too.

He brought blankets to one family, a lamp to another, a coat to one family, a flowerpot to another. To all those people living so far from home, he seemed like an elf who turned up with the very thing they needed.

One day he arrived in a truck—with a shiny new bike for Mevan.

He had seen her when others hadn't.

And his gift made Mevan feel a hundred feet tall.

Mevan loved the wind in her hair. She loved the squeak of the brakes. But more than anything, she loved feeling like just one of the kids.

A year later, Mevan's parents got the good news that there was a new home waiting for them. A home in a country where they would be safe, where they would never have to leave.

Mevan and her family had to leave in such a hurry that she never got a chance to say goodbye to Egbert.

But she never forgot the feeling
that bike gave her.
  And she never forgot the man
who taught her how big a small act of
kindness can be.

Arjen van der Zee

EPILOGUE

After she grew up, Mevan went back to the land of figs and honeysuckle and retraced all the steps her family had taken when they were forced to leave Kurdistan. She saw her aunts and uncles, her grandmother and her grandfather. But the grocer was gone. So were many others who'd disappeared when they'd had to flee Kurdistan.

When Mevan arrived in the Netherlands, she asked around about Egbert. She'd thought of him often through the years; whenever she'd been sad or lonely, she reminded herself that there are always kind people in the world. So she put his picture on the internet. "Can anyone help me find this man?" she wrote.

Within minutes, a hundred people had shared her message. Then a thousand. Then ten thousand. Then a hundred thousand. In just one day she was knocking at his front door!

Their story started something special. People all over the world shared stories about the kind things that strangers had done for them. And then something even more wonderful happened. In a world where there are many people running from war, from hunger, from hatred, people everywhere, of every age, asked themselves: What's one kind thing I can do?

Author's Note

Millions of children all over the world are refugees like I was. As I write, there are more than forty-three million children who have had to leave their homes because it isn't safe for them to stay there. They leave behind their toys, their friends, their schools—and may never get to see their grandparents, aunts or uncles, and cousins again. Sometimes children are separated from their parents. And, like our family, refugees are often sent from one country to another, not welcome no matter where they go.

Refugees sometimes live in tents where they have no water or electricity. Or they live in crowded apartments or houses, hiding from people who want to send them back to the dangerous places where they used to live. They may be living far away in another country, or they might be living nearby.

Our family went from Kurdistan to Turkey, Azerbaijan, Russia, the Netherlands, and finally the United Kingdom. Over the course of four years, we traveled by car, by boat, by foot, by van, by ferry, by plane, and by train. In Russia, we were robbed by people who pretended to help us and left us stranded; we told the police but instead of helping us, they ripped up our refugee papers. Sometimes we were even put in jail.

We eventually escaped to the Netherlands, but there wasn't enough money for my father to come too. He had to stay in Russia for four more years and I wasn't sure I'd ever see him again.

Finally, our family was reunited in the United Kingdom, where we found a safe and happy home. But there are many times when I still feel like an outsider. I am proud of my parents for their bravery and proud of myself and my family for the way we made a home for ourselves no matter where we were. Being a refugee will always be a part of who I am—and it's made me aware of the ways all of us can feel like outsiders, no matter where we come from.

But it's also taught me about the miraculous power of kindness: It was always the small kindnesses that stuck with me as I was growing up. One small and generous act made me feel noticed. After all the ways in which the world had told me that I didn't matter, thanks to Egbert and this gift, at least for a little while, I could be like every other kid—just a little girl riding her bike.

—Mevan Babakar